Unity Birdhouses

by Frankie Buckley

Leisure Arts Inc.
Maumelle , Arkansas

HOW TO READ THE CHART

The chart is made up of a key and a gridded design where each square represents a stitch. The symbols in the key tell which floss color to use for each stitch in the chart. The following headings and symbols are given:

X — Cross Stitch
DMC — DMC color number
1/4 X — Quarter Stitch
1/2 X — Half Cross Stitch
B'ST — Backstitch
ANC. — Anchor color number
COLOR — the name given to the floss color in this chart

A square filled with a color and a symbol should be worked as a Cross Stitch.

A triangle should be worked as a **Quarter Stitch**.

A square containing a colored symbol should be worked as a **Half Cross Stitch**.

A straight line should be worked as a **Backstitch**.

A large dot listed near the end of the key should be worked as a **French Knot**.

Sometimes the symbol for a **Cross Stitch** may be partially covered when a **Backstitch** crosses the square. Refer to the background color to determine the floss color.

HOW TO STITCH

Always work **Cross Stitches**, **Quarter Stitches**, and **Half Cross Stitches** first and then add the **Backstitch** and **French Knots.**

Cross Stitch (X): For horizontal rows, work stitches in two journeys ***(Fig. 1)***. For vertical rows, complete each stitch as shown ***(Fig. 2)***.

Fig. 1

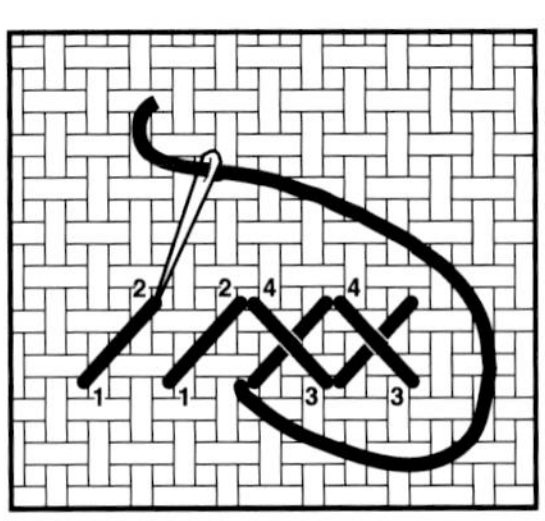

Fig. 2

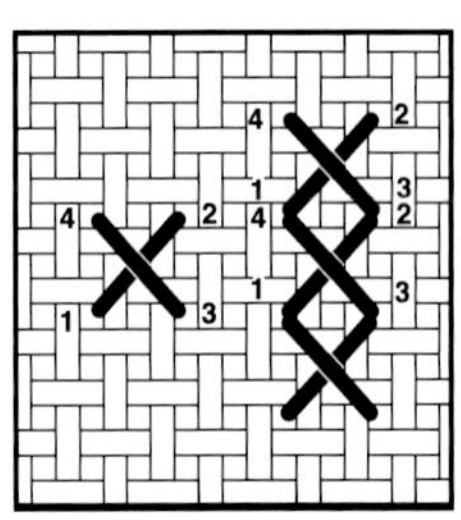

Quarter Stitch (1/4X): Come up at 1 ***(Fig. 3)***, then split fabric thread to go down at 2.

Fig. 3

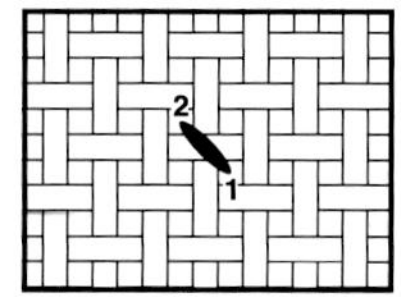

Half Cross Stitch (1/2X): This stitch is one journey of the Cross Stitch and is worked from lower left to upper right as shown in **Fig. 4**.

Fig. 4

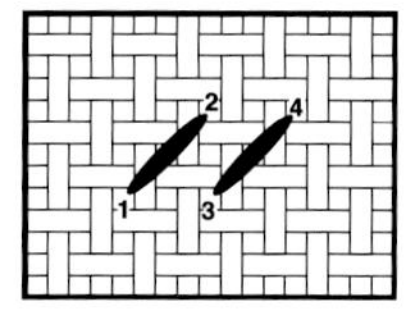

Backstitch (B'ST): For outlines and details, Backstitch should be worked after the design has been completed ***(Fig. 5)***.

Fig. 5

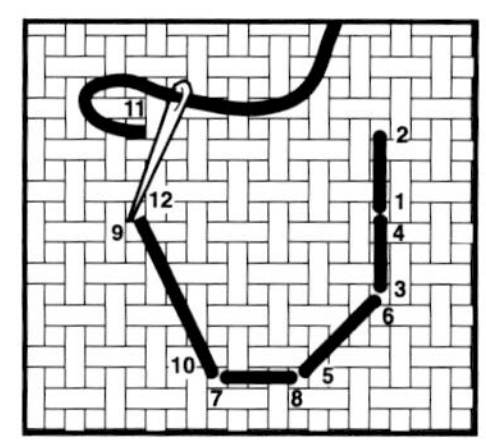

French Knot: Bring needle up at 1. Wrap floss once around needle. Insert needle at 2, tighten knot, and pull needle through fabric, holding floss until it must be released ***(Fig. 6)***. For a larger knot, use more floss strands; wrap only once.

Fig. 6

STITCHING TIP

Working over Two Fabric Threads

When working over two fabric threads, the stitches should be placed so that vertical fabric threads support each stitch. Make sure that the first Cross Stitch is placed on the fabric with stitch 1-2 beginning and ending where a vertical fabric thread crosses over a horizontal fabric thread ***(Fig. 7)***.

Fig. 7

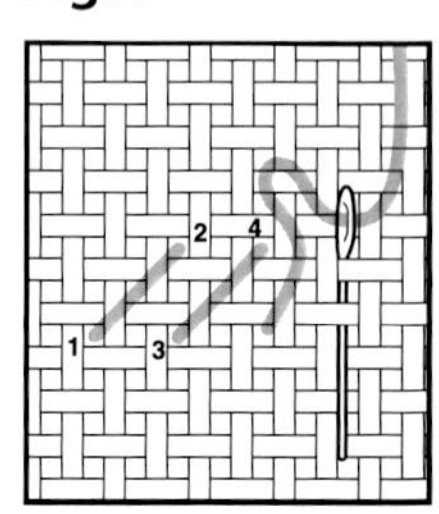

Unity Birdhouses

X	DMC	1/4X	1/2X	B'ST	ANC.	COLOR
5	221				897	shell pink
	312				979	navy
¢	322				978	lt navy
∇	334				977	dk blue
	336			†	150	dk navy
Δ	347				1025	dk salmon
C	469				267	dk green
M	470	M			267	green
4	471				266	lt green
Λ	472	Λ			253	vy lt green
G	646	G			8581	beige grey
	647				1040	lt beige grey
	648				900	vy lt beige grey
	730				845	dk olive
	*730				845	dk olive
O	732		+		281	olive
+	*732				281	olive
	733				280	lt olive
	*733				280	lt olive
⊥	734				279	vy lt olive
	*734				279	vy lt olive
7	746	7			275	cream
H	777					lt maroon
T	814	T			45	maroon
	844			★	1041	vy dk beige grey
⊞	918	⊞		★	341	rust
⋈	921	⋈			1003	lt rust
■	934			†	862	avocado
S	936	S			269	vy dk green
◀	3031				905	dk brown
⋈	3045				888	lt gold
e	3046				887	gold
◇	3047				852	dk gold

X	DMC	1/4X	1/2X	B'ST	ANC.	COLOR
#	3072				847	grey
	3328				1024	salmon
✳	3712				1023	lt salmon
Z	3755	Z			140	blue
−	3756	−			1037	vy lt blue
★	*3781		★		904	brown
Q	3831				29	dk pink
E	3832				28	pink
	3833				26	lt pink
6	3841				9159	lt blue
3	3853	3			1003	copper
+	3854	+			313	lt copper
	3855				311	yellow
☆	3865			†	2	off white
●	844				1041	vy dk beige grey Fr. Knot
●	3031				905	dk brown Fr. Knot
●	3865				2	off white Fr. Knot

Pink area indicates last row of previous section of design.

* Use **1** strand of floss.

† DMC 336 for blue bird, blue birdhouse, and patriotic birdhouse. DMC 934 for white birdhouse. DMC 3865 for all birds' eyes.

★ DMC 844 for grey bird, blue bird's feet, red bird's beak, blue birdhouse, white birdhouse, and opening of patriotic birdhouse. DMC 918 for rust birdhouse and patriotic birdhouse.

Design was stitched on a 19 1/2" x 16 1/2" piece of 28 count Antique White Cashel Linen® (design size 13 1/2" x 10 1/4") over two fabric threads. Two strands of floss were used for Cross Stitch and 1 strand for Half Cross Stitch, Backstitch, and French Knots except where noted in key. It was custom framed.

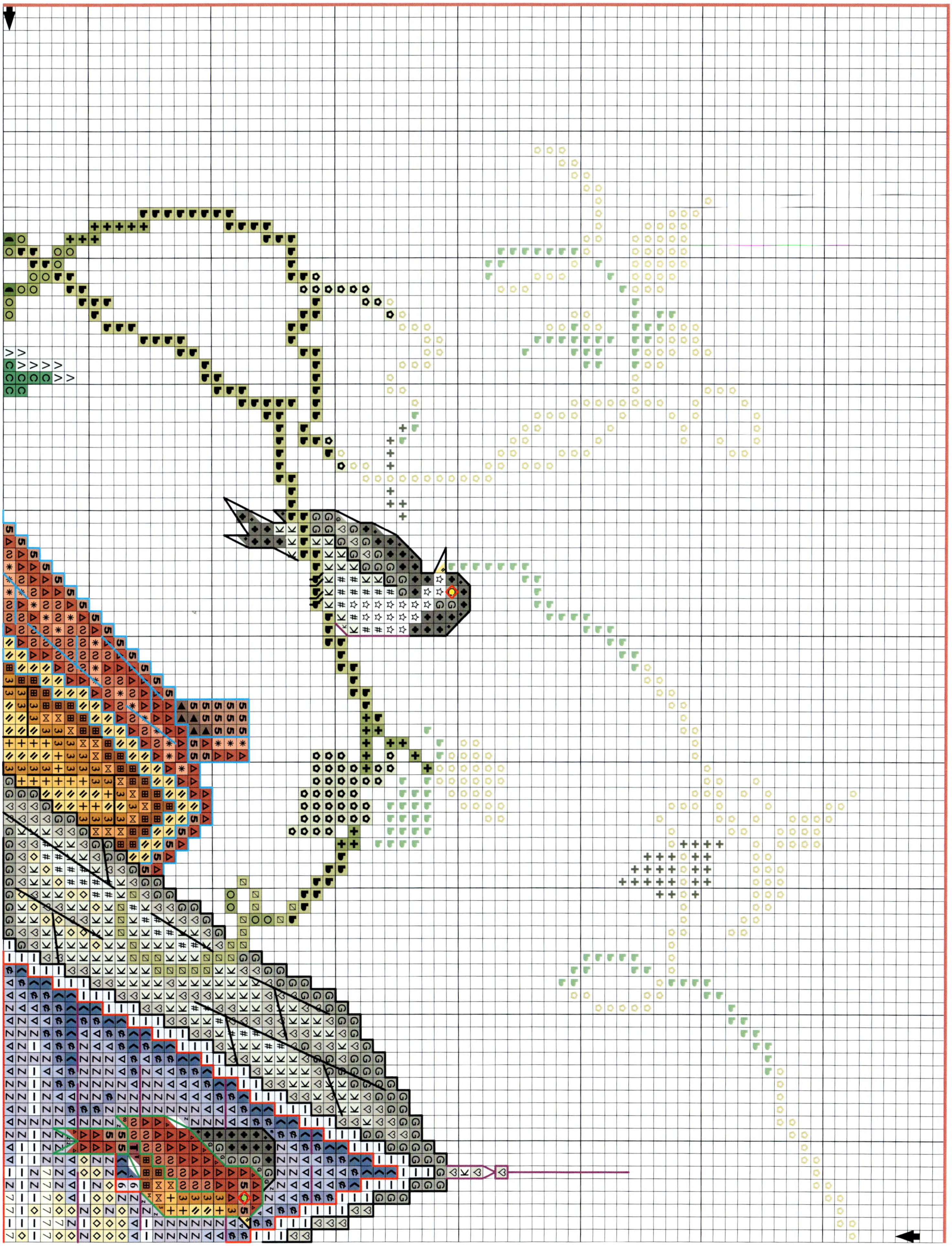

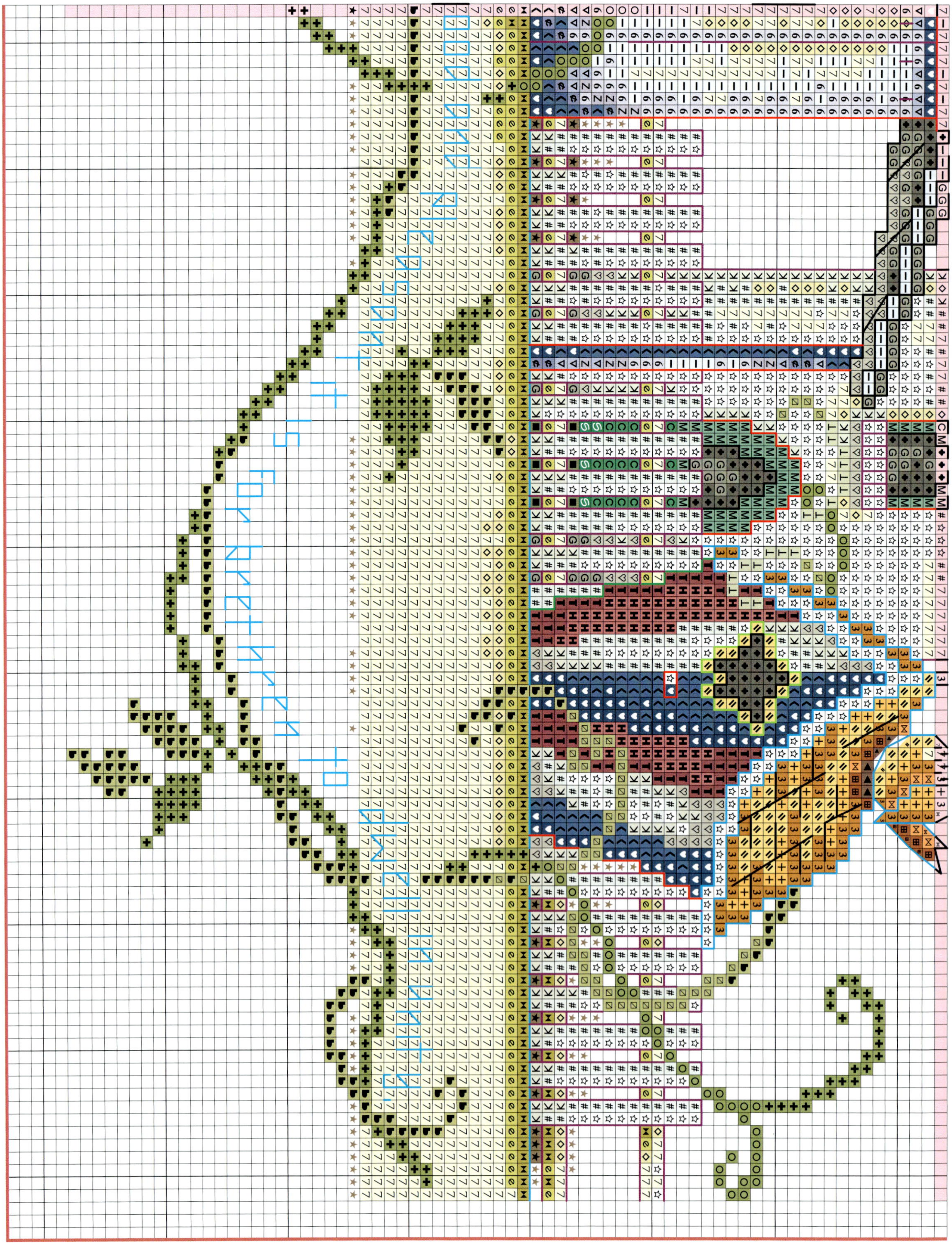

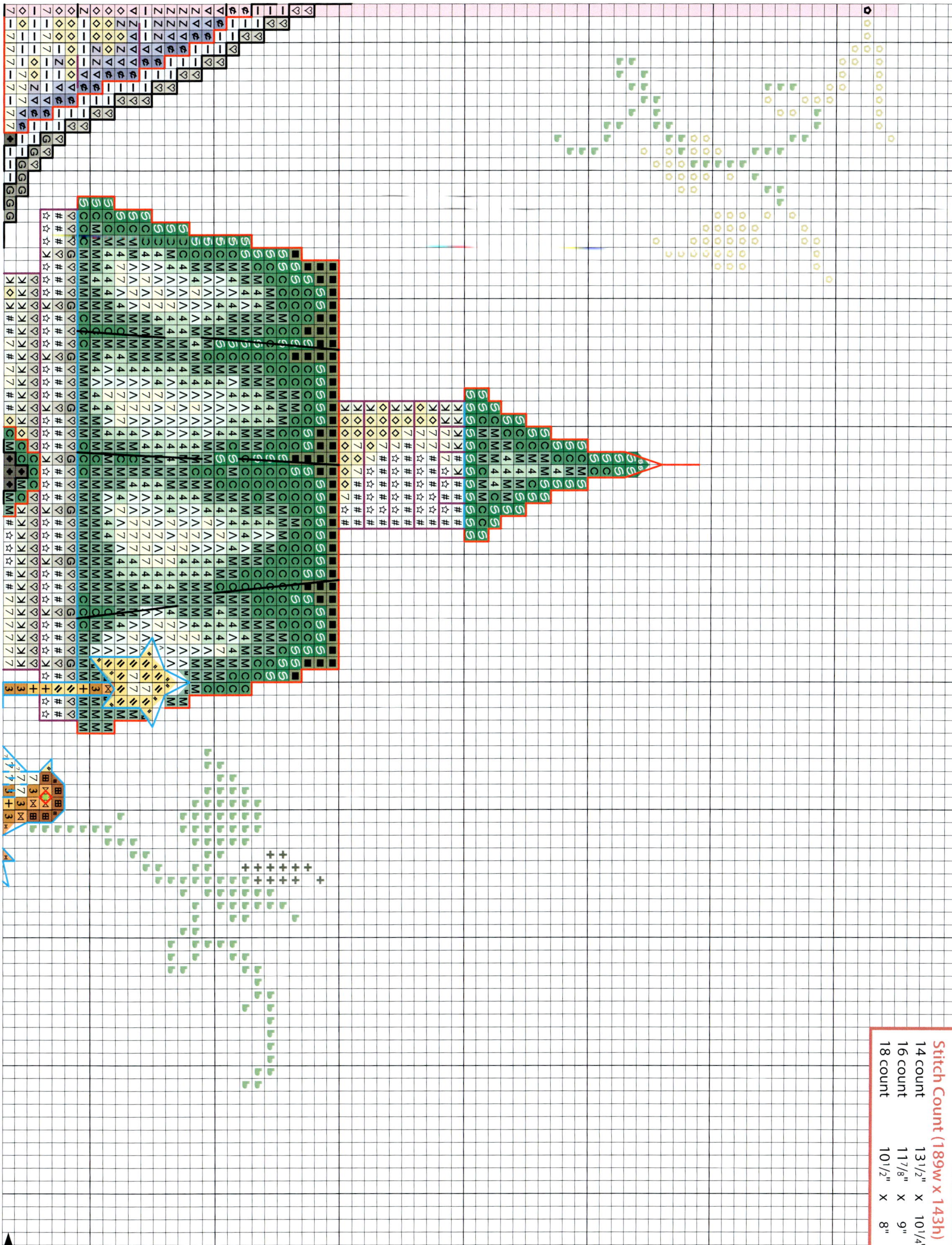

Stitch Count (189w x 143h)

14 count	$13^1/_2$"	x	$10^1/_4$"
16 count	$11^7/_8$"	x	9"
18 count	$10^1/_2$"	x	8"

Show us what you're working on!

Share your project photos with us on social media.
Tag us @leisureartsinc or use #leisurearts

Made in U.S.A.

We have made every effort to ensure that these instructions are accurate and complete. We cannot, however, be responsible for human error, typographical mistakes, or variations in individual work.Needlework adaptation by Carol Emmer.

Fabric provided courtesy of Zweigart®.
Embroidery floss provided courtesy of The DMC Corporation.

Production Team: Writer – Karen Jackson; Graphic Artist – Karen F. Allbright; Editorial Writer – Suzie Puckett; and Photo Stylist – Cassie Newsome.